Cuisine Tybeen

PALMETTO
PUBLISHING

Charleston, SC
www.PalmettoPublishing.com

Cuisine Tybeen

First Edition

Hardcover ISBN: 979-8-88590-997-6
Paperback ISBN: 979-8-88590-998-3
eBook ISBN: 979-8-88590-999-0

Cuisine Tybeen

VOLUME ONE

NASSAB A. AHMADIE

This is my invariable advice to people: Learn how to cook, try new recipes, learn from your mistakes, be fearless, and above all have fun!

– *Julia Child*

Photography and design by Nassab Ahmadie

Editing by Gabriella Williams

v

Dedication

I dedicate this book (the first of a series, hopefully) first and foremost to my three children: Serena, Alyssar, and Sami. My magnificent three! You are my greatest accomplishment in life. I am blessed that you are mine!

My second dedication comes from my heart to Ziad, my husband—the healer, the helper, and the supporter of all my 101 careers, roles, and ambitions. I am so happy you found me.

This book is also dedicated to my mother, who patiently and lovingly introduced me to the world of cooking. She taught me the ins and outs of the kitchen and never used anything other than her own judgment to measure her ingredients. And to my mother-in-law, who opened my eyes and my taste buds to new and different flavors.

Last but not least, I devote this book to all of the Lebanese mothers who have struggled in the midst of such chaotic times. With a pandemic, a catastrophic explosion, the loss of work, a lack of financial stability, and the restriction of access to food and medical supplies, Lebanon has faced immense suffering. Mothers who have struggled to put food on the table yet kept a smile on your face, this is for you.

Lebanese people are incredibly tenacious. They fight and hope through adversity; they cheer and rise through injustice; they have open hearts and open doors. I pray that God will strengthen their resilience and help them journey into a better future.

The proceeds from this book will be donated to Beytna Charitable Foundation to benefit struggling communities in Mount Lebanon. More information is available online and through social media. Links and websites will be provided at the end of the book.

I sincerely hope that you will enjoy making these recipes; it has been an honor to write them. Thank you for reading. There will be more to follow.

Sincerely,

Nassab A. Ahmadie

Growing up in a Lebanese home blessed me with fond memories of gatherings around the dining room table and in the kitchen, where I watched and helped my mother prepare delicious Lebanese food. It wasn't until a few years ago, when my eldest daughter was preparing to go to college and live on her own, that I realized that I could share with my children the joys of food and the rewards of preparing it yourself.

While putting together this collection, I tried to focus on recipes that were simple to prepare and used easily attainable ingredients. Additionally, I wanted to ensure that these meals were healthy and accessible to those with dietary restrictions without compromising flavor or taste. Cuisine Tybeen ("delicious cuisine" in Arabic) is an assortment of bright, fresh, and invigorating meals.

The recipes I have curated create a broad spectrum of flavors for those who want to delve into the rich palette of Lebanese cuisine. A few dishes originate from a variety of other cultures but have been reimagined with distinct Lebanese flair. Some of these recipes incorporate spices that are not widely available throughout the United States. All of these ingredients can be purchased online from well-established sellers and retailers.

This collection is divided into four sections: soups and salads, main dishes, side dishes, and sweets. Each section begins with a preview of the recipes within.

While the prep time for the soups and salads may appear slightly lengthy, you will find that once you have your mise en place, putting the recipe into action will be smooth and quick. In my experience, these items are also usually best served soon after they are assembled, and therefore I often prepare, measure, and assemble the ingredients ahead of time.

The main dishes I have selected sometimes require additional preparation ahead of time. Much like the salads, these recipes are often labor intensive when it comes to gathering and preparing the ingredients, although the actual cooking process can take far less time.

With soups, I have found that sometimes it is best to let them sit covered on the stove after they have been cooked to allow the soup to thicken and bind. I would recommend trying this if you think your soup is too watery or thin. Typically, an additional resting period of 15 to 30 minutes is sufficient.

Desserts can also be given time to settle in the oven. If you want a more golden hue on top, turn the oven off and leave the dish untouched for around 15 to 20 minutes. This time can vary depending on the strength of your oven.

Another piece of advice I like to give, especially to beginners, is to stock your kitchen with high-quality utensils. A reliable kitchen knife that can last for decades is well worth the cost. Conversely, your daily pots and pans (especially the nonstick or aluminum brands that get scuffed, burned, or scratched through the years) are more easily replaced.

All of these recipes use precise measurements (barring the occasional garnish recommendation and the salt and pepper, which can be adjusted to taste). I used to struggle to follow recipes that used vague instructions. What exactly is a medium onion or a large tomato? My personal frustrations with these kinds of instructions have shaped how I have listed ingredients in this book. Each recipe has clear measurements, and if you find that some portions are left over, many of them can be easily reused in other dishes, or you can use the opportunity to flex your creativity.

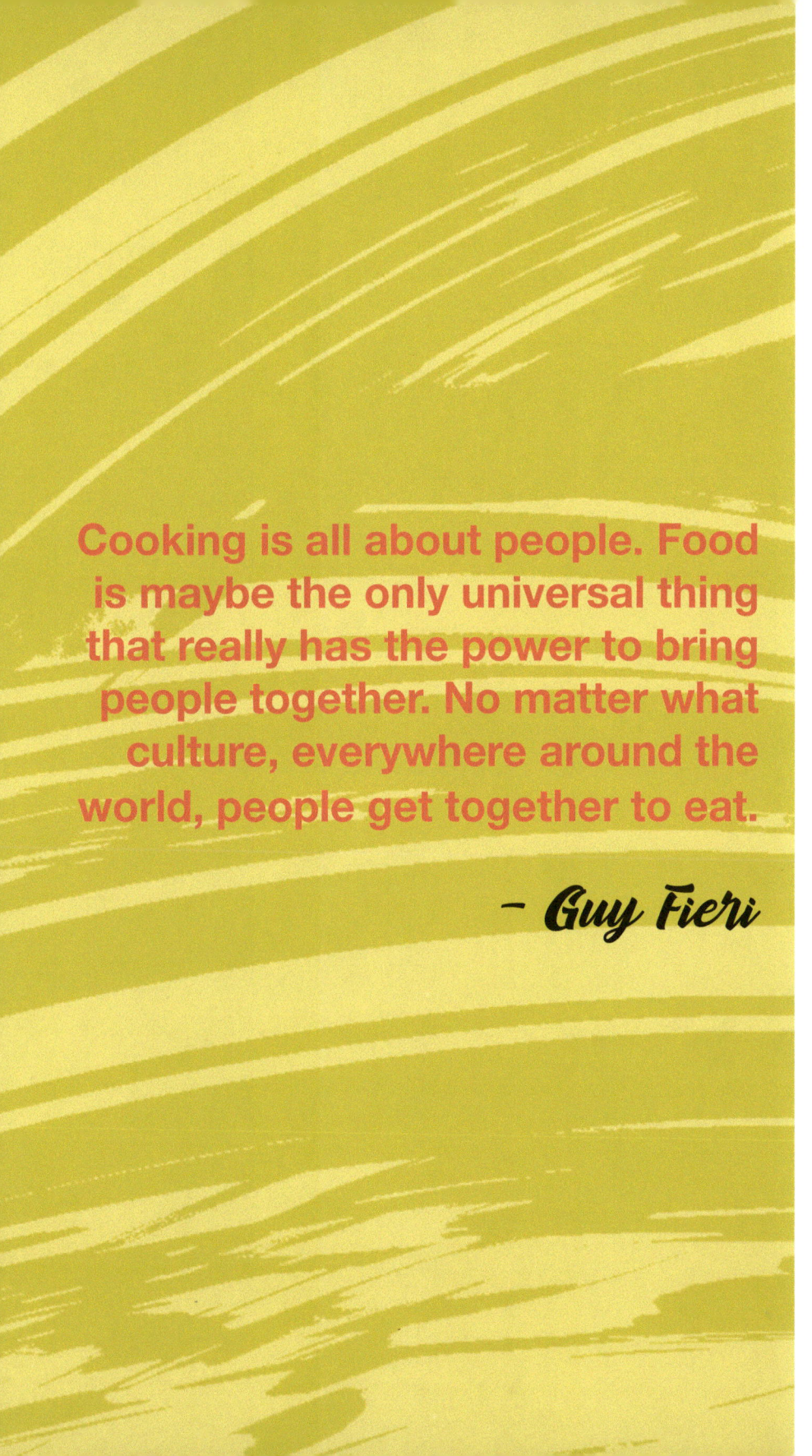

Cooking is all about people. Food is maybe the only universal thing that really has the power to bring people together. No matter what culture, everywhere around the world, people get together to eat.

– Guy Fieri

INTRODUCTION

SOUPS AND SALADS

Healthy and Fullfilling
 Fresh and Vibrant

x

01. Lentil Soup

This simple, colorful soup is packed with nutrients and flavor. It is vegan, gluten-free, low fat, and can be stored safely to eat throughout the week, which makes it perfect for meal prep.

02. Vegetable, Beef, and Rice Soup

A hearty and filling soup that is made to eat fresh. This recipe is packed with flavor, carbs, and protein. If stored properly in a tightly sealed container, this dish can remain fresh for up to two days.

03. Chicken Taco Soup

Inspired by Lebanese cuisine, this recipe diverges from the traditional Mexican dish to bring new, authentic flavors to your palate. It is a great blend of healthy vegetables, meat, and carbs and is easy to prepare.

04. Tabouleh

The most colorful of this collection by far! This famous Lebanese dish is easily made and easily devoured. The key here is to chop finely and mince well to best incorporate those rich, clean flavors that will make your mouth water.

05. Cabbage Salad

Say hello to the Lebanese version of American coleslaw! After trying this, you will not look twice at mayo-filled, bland-tasting, restaurant-made slaw ever again. This recipe is the perfect blend of bold and exotic color to satisfy your taste buds!

06. Fatoush

This dish has all things vegetables blended together with sumac, lemon, and extra-virgin olive oil dressing. It can be topped with baked or fried crumbs of pita bread. This recipe is not labor intensive and involves all the colorful flavors of tabbouleh.

Red Lentil Soup

This soup is velvety, slightly textured, and the ultimate form of comfort food. It doesn't sacrifice flavor for warmth and ease. A good pairing with this soup is pita bread or your choice of thick cracker.

INGREDIENTS

- 2 cups lentils
- 1 cup finely chopped carrots
- 2 cups finely chopped yellow squash
- 2 cups finely chopped onions
- 2 tablespoons minced garlic
- 1 cup tomato sauce
- ½ teaspoon cumin
- ½ teaspoon coriander powder

- 1½ teaspoons paprika
- 2 dried bay leaves
- ½ cup lemon juice
- 1 teaspoon salt
- ½ teaspoon allspice seasoning
- ¼ cup canola oil
- 8 cups water or vegetable stock

Nonvegan option: Add a chicken bouillon cube or 1 teaspoon of chicken bouillon powder to the water or substitute water with 8 cups of chicken stock.

4-5 PEOPLE 45-1hr VEGAN GLUTEN FREE

PREPARATION

1. Cover the lentils in water and bring to a boil. Be sure to scoop out the foam and debris that forms on top. Let simmer for about 10 minutes.

2. Begin sautéing the chopped onions.

3. After a few minutes, once the onions are golden and translucent, add the garlic to the pan.

4. Wait a few minutes, then add the carrots, followed by the squash.

5. Cover and let simmer for a maximum of 10 minutes.

6. While the vegetables sauté, drain the boiled lentils.

7. Place the lentils and the vegetable mix into a pot.

8. Add the tomato sauce, cumin, coriander powder, paprika, allspice, bay leaves, lemon juice, and water, and then bring to a boil.

9. Lower the heat and let the mixture simmer until the vegetables and lentils are well cooked. This should not take more than 10 minutes.

10. Taste and leave covered on the stove for another 10 to 15 minutes, then serve.

Vegetable Beef and Rice Soup

4-5 PEOPLE **45-1hr** **LOW FAT**

PREPARATION

1. Sauté the onions and the garlic in the canola oil for a maximum of 10 minutes. Wait until the onions turn translucent or golden.

2. Add the meat, salt, black pepper, and shawarma spice.

3. Stir, cover, and cook for 2 to 3 minutes.

4. Add the tomato paste, onions, garlic, squash, and carrots and let the mixture cook for up to 10 minutes. Be sure to stir periodically.

5. Bring the mixture to a boil.

6. After the rice is done and taste tested, turn off the heat and add the ¼ cup of freshly chopped parsley.

7. Leave covered for 30 minutes. Do not stir. This will allow the soup to thicken a little and for the meat and the vegetables to tenderize.

This soup is perfect for those cold winter days when the kids come back from school hungry and ready to eat. The blend of vegetables makes the dish bright, colorful, and flavorful, while the shawarma spices provide a distinctly satisfying taste that gives the soup's flavor more dimension. This recipe is made to eat fresh, though the soup can be stored for up to a day or two without spoiling.

INGREDIENTS

- ¼ cup canola oil
- 2 cups finely chopped onions
- 1 tablespoon finely chopped garlic
- 2 cups finely chopped squash
- 2 cups finely chopped carrots
- 2 cups shawarma-style chopped steak (filet mignon or London broil)
- 3 teaspoons salt
- 2½ teaspoons shawarma spice
- A sprinkle of black pepper
- 1 tablespoon tomato paste
- 1 cup long-grain rice
- 10 cups water
- 1 bouillon beef or chicken
- ¼ cup finely chopped parsley

8-10 PEOPLE

45-1hr

LOW FAT

Chicken Taco Soup

This hearty, filling, and robust recipe includes all the Mexican spices and herbs that awaken your palate, while also using Mediterranean ingredients to liven up a dish that is familiar to many.

INGREDIENTS

- ¼ cup canola oil
- 1 cup finely chopped onions
- 2 cups finely chopped peppers
- 2 teaspoons salt
- 1 teaspoon black pepper
- 1 can (15 ounces) black beans, drained
- 1 can (15¼ ounces) sweet whole-kernel corn, drained
- 1 tablespoon taco seasoning
- 4 cups strained tomatoes
- 4 cups chicken broth
- 1 cup of your choice of spoon-friendly pasta (i.e., thin vermicelli noodles broken into small pieces)

OPTIONAL INGREDIENTS

- Finely chopped jalapeños or red peppers (for additional flavor and heat, adjust to taste)

PREPARATION

1. Heat the oil in a large pot over medium heat.

2. Add the onion and peppers, season with salt and pepper, and cook for 5 minutes.

3. If incorporating additional jalapeños or red peppers, add them to the pot and stir until incorporated.

4. Add the black beans, corn, tomato sauce, chicken, and taco seasoning. Stir until incorporated.

5. Add the chicken broth and cook on medium to high heat. Bring to a simmer. Cook covered for 10 minutes.

6. Taste and add additional salt and pepper if needed.

7. Stir, add the pasta, and cook covered for another 5 minutes.

8. Stir again, turn off the heat, and leave covered for 5 minutes.

9. Serve hot.

Tabouleh

PREPARATION

1. Start by rinsing the parsley well. Lay the herb on a towel or in a strainer and organize into bunches. Gather a handful at a time and cut off the long stems. Dispose of the stems before you mince.

2. Rinse the tomatoes, onions, and mint and then finely chop them.

3. Combine the minced parsley, tomatoes, onions, and mint in a large bowl.

4. On the side, soak the burghul in water for a few minutes in a small bowl. If using quinoa as a substitute, prepare in the same way.

5. Add the lemon juice, olive oil, seven spice blend, salt and pepper to the bowl.

6. Drain the burghul wheat after it is soft and absorbed and mix into the tabbouleh mixture. If using a gluten-free substitute, prepare it the same way.

7. Adjust the salt and lemon to taste and serve.

This recipe brings all of the deliciousness of tabouleh to the table. I'm talking about the juicy, colorful tabouleh with enough extra virgin olive oil, lemon, and tomato juice to perfectly diversify your palate and refresh your taste buds. This dish is made to be eaten alone as a side or to be used as a dip for your choice of protein or homemade french fries.

INGREDIENTS

- 4 cups chopped parsley
- 3 cups chopped tomatoes
- ¼ cup chopped fresh mint or 1 tablespoon of dried mint
- ¾ cup chopped green onions/scallions
- ½ cup extra-virgin olive oil
- ⅓ cup dry burghul (substitute with ⅓ cup quinoa for a gluten-free option)
- ½ cup lemon juice
- 1½ teaspoons salt
- 1 teaspoon seven-spice blend

8-10 PEOPLE

45-1hr

VEGAN

Cabbage Salad

4-5 PEOPLE **VEGAN** **45-1hr** **GLUTEN FREE**

The dressing for this recipe is wonderfully simple and yet rich in flavor. It utilizes the traditional ingredients of garlic, extra-virgin olive oil, and lemon and adds new spices to enhance the taste and robustness of the vegetables. This dish is most flavorful the day after it is prepared, once there has been enough time for the ingredients to soak thoroughly into the cabbage.

INGREDIENTS

- 3 cups shredded or finely chopped cabbage
- 2 cups finely chopped tomatoes
- ¼ cup chopped dried mint
- 1 cup finely chopped carrots
- 1 cup peeled, finely chopped radishes
- 1 cup peeled, finely chopped cucumbers
- ⅔ cup lemon juice
- ⅔ cup extra-virgin olive oil
- 1 teaspoon salt
- A sprinkle of black pepper

PREPARATION

1. Rinse and chop all the vegetables and mix thoroughly in a large bowl.

2. Add the lemon juice, olive oil, salt, pepper, and dried mint and mix again.

3. Once the ingredients are well incorporated, taste. If satisfied, serve cold.

4. For maximum flavor, allow the dish to settle in the fridge overnight and then serve.

Fatoush

A fresh mix of greens that is full of sharp, tangy tastes. The name fattoush derives from fatteh, which means "crumbs." This recipe is similar to tabbouleh but doesn't require as much intense mincing and is more often served as a stand-alone dish.

INGREDIENTS

- 4 cups chopped lettuce
- 1 cup chopped tomatoes
- 1 cup chopped cucumbers
- 1 cup chopped radishes
- 1 cup chopped carrots
- 1 cup chopped peppers
- 1 cup chopped parsley
- ½ cup chopped fresh mint or 2 tablespoons dry mint flakes
- ½ cup chopped green or white onions
- 1 cup purslane leaves (optional if unavailable)
- ¾ cup extra-virgin olive oil
- ½ cup lemon
- 2 tablespoons sumac
- 1 teaspoon salt
- ¼ teaspoon fresh black pepper
- 2 cups fried or baked pita chips

8-10 PEOPLE

45-1hr

VEGAN

PREPARATION

1. All the vegetables except for the onions can be prepared ahead of time if desired.

2. Mix the chopped lettuce, tomatoes, cucumbers, radishes, carrots, peppers, parsley, mint, onions, and purslane leaves together in a bowl until the vegetables appear to be evenly distributed.

3. Mix the extra-virgin olive oil, lemon, sumac, salt, and fresh black pepper together in a separate dish and ensure they are well incorporated.

4. When both the vegetables and wet ingredients are mixed to your satisfaction, pour the dressing over the vegetables.

5. Mix the vegetables and dressing well.

6. Top the dish with the pita chips and serve immediately.

MAIN DISHES

A unique, eclectic, and healthy variety for the whole ►►► family to enjoy.

01. Chicken and Potatoes with Curry over Plain Rice

A dinner that will awaken your taste buds with its variety of spices. This dish is packed with carbs and protein for a striking, fun, and fulfilling taste. It is low fat and perfect for meal prep.

02. Beef Stew

This rich and hearty stew with Lebanese influences is suitable for lunch and dinner. It can be prepared in advance for those on the go and will remain fresh for a few days if stored properly.

03. Kafta and Potatoes

Enjoy a traditional, satisfying meat-and-potatoes combination that is simple, tasty, and a staple in Lebanese cuisine. The parsley (which is dense with vitamin K and vitamin C) and special spices in the meat give it a unique taste and pack on protein.

Main Dishes

04. Kibbeh

This dish is yet another staple in Lebanese cuisine. The meat and burghul (cracked wheat) mix well with spices and herbs to create an exotic blend of flavors. It is apt for large gatherings as well as meal prep. It stores well when frozen and can be baked after freezing to serve to friends or family.

05. Loubeh Bzeit

This dish provides a refreshing new way to flavor green beans. This is a traditional recipe in Lebanese culture that has been passed down through many generations. Loubie bzeit is often found at family gatherings, whether it is served as a casual side or as a part of a feast. This recipe is vegan, although it can pair wonderfully with any meat.

06. Mussakhan Tortilla Rolls

This dish is ideal for lunches on the go but can also be served at dinner. This Mediterranean recipe is a favorite among kids and is a good way to expose them to new flavors and spices. Musakhan tortilla rolls are also low fat and a great vessel for getting in your daily protein.

Chicken and Potatoes with Curry over Plain Rice

This is a popular Mediterranean recipe that has an abundance of variations across the world. It is hearty, filling, and dense with flavor. This dish can also be served without rice, if desired.

INGREDIENTS

- 2 tablespoons finely chopped garlic
- 4 cups chopped russet potatoes
- 4 cups chopped chicken
- ⅓ cup canola oil
- 2½ teaspoons salt
- 2½ teaspoons curry powder
- 1 teaspoon black pepper
- 3 tablespoons tomato paste
- 7 cups water or chicken stock
- 1 teaspoon red pepper (optional)

INGREDIENTS FOR RICE

- 1 cup basmati or any long-grain rice
- 1 teaspoon salted butter
- 2¼ cups water
- 1 teaspoon salt

6-8 PEOPLE   45-1hr   LOW FAT

PREPARATION

1. Add the canola oil to a pot on medium heat.

2. Sauté the garlic in the hot canola oil.

3. After 1 to 2 minutes, add the chicken.

4. Incorporate the curry powder, black pepper, and salt with the chicken.

5. Mix and cover the pot and cook for 5 minutes.

6. Then, add the potatoes, the tomato paste, and the water.

7. Mix together, cover, and let cook on medium to high heat for 10 minutes.

8. Adjust the salt to taste, cover the pot, and leave on the stovetop for about 15 minutes.

9. Serve over plain rice.

RICE PREPARATION

1. Melt the butter in a separate dish until it is a liquid.

2. Rinse the rice in a strainer, then drain and add to the butter.

3. Pour the water into a pot and add salt.

4. Bring to a boil on medium to high heat and add the rice and butter. Allow the rice to cook for 6 to 8 minutes.

5. Then, lower the heat and let simmer for another 6 to 8 minutes.

6. Turn the heat off and cover.

7. Let the rice rest for about 30 minutes to make sure it is well cooked.

Beef Stew

4-5 PEOPLE

45-1hr

LOW FAT

PREPARATION

1. In a dutch-oven (or stockpot), sear the beef on each side for a few minutes. When the outer surface of the meat has an even, rich brown exterior, remove and set aside.

2. Scrape the fond from the pot and add the onions, garlic, potatoes, and carrots.

3. Let the mix cook for about five minutes. Stir periodically to ensure the ingredients form a firm exterior.

4. Add the tomato paste and flour into the mixture. Stir until fully incorporated.

5. Once the mix is evenly coated, add the meat, salt, pepper, thyme, basil, rosemary, wine and beef stock. Stir and then cover.

This simple, warm, and rich stew is perfect for lunch or dinner and is the ultimate comfort meal. It has an excellent balance of hearty and fulfilling flavors. It is perfect for meal prep and will remain fresh for a few days if stored properly.

INGREDIENTS

- 2 cups cubed beef chuck roast
- 2 cups cubed carrots
- 2 cups cubed russet potatoes
- 2 cups cubed onions
- ½ cup canola oil
- 2 tablespoons finely chopped garlic
- 1 teaspoon salt
- 1 teaspoon black pepper
- 1 teaspoon thyme
- 1 teaspoon rosemary
- 1 teaspoon basil
- ¼ cup all-purpose flour
- 1 tablespoon tomato paste
- 1½ cups of your choice of red wine
- 3 cups beef stock

6. Bring to a boil and let it cook for 4-5 minutes. Stir and then re-cover.

7. Lower the heat and let the stew simmer for 10-20 minutes. Stir occasionally.

8. Before turning off the heat, check to see if the potatoes and carrots are cooked by piercing a few pieces with a fork. The vegetables should slide off of the fork easily when cooked properly.

9. Turn off the heat and let the stew rest, covered, for 30 minutes before serving.

Kafta and Potatoes

This Lebanese recipe is popular among all age groups. It is ideal for large family gatherings or events and is bound to impress your guests. The rich spices, tender meat, and well-seasoned vegetables make a toothsome combination you won't soon forget.

INGREDIENTS

- 3 cups (24 ounces) ground beef or lamb
- 2 cups chopped onion
- 1 teaspoon salt
- 1 teaspoon seven-spice blend
- 1 cup finely chopped parsley
- 4 tablespoons canola oil
- 3 large russet potatoes, rondelle cut
- ½ teaspoon Himalayan salt
- ¼ teaspoon pepper
- 2 medium tomatoes, rondelle cut

INGREDIENTS FOR SAUCE

- 2 tablespoons tomato paste
- ½ teaspoon salt
- 4 cups water

PREPARATION

1. Mix the meat, onions, salt, seven-spice blend, and parsley in an electric mixer, using a flat beater, or mix by hand.

2. Form the blend into small patties.

3. In a separate pan, add the canola oil and let it warm a little bit.

4. Then, over medium to high heat, add the meat patties one by one.

5. Allow the patties to cook for a few minutes on each side.

6. Once they have browned, remove and set aside. These are not to be eaten at this point. The inside is still raw.

7. In the same pan, add the potatoes, salt, and pepper.

8. Cook the potatoes in the same way you prepared the meat. Give each side about 5 minutes in the pan to brown and crispen.

9. After each side has been heated, remove the potatoes and set them aside.

10. In an oven-safe tray (lined with aluminum foil for easier cleaning later), layer the meat, potatoes, and tomatoes in whatever order you prefer.

11. Pour the tomato-based sauce over the tray, cover with aluminum foil, and bake for 45 minutes to 1 hour at 400°F. Uncover after 30 minutes. If necessary, rotate the tray to ensure that the dish is being heated evenly in the oven.

PREPARATION FOR SAUCE

1. Dissolve the tomato paste and salt in 4 cups of water. The sauce will cook in theoven once it has been added to the tray.

Kibbeh

4-5 PEOPLE **1-1.5 hr** **LOW FAT**

This dish's durability makes it ideal for moms like me, who want to make meals in advance and save time when prepping dinner. Kibbeh can be prepared in a variety of ways. The first method of preparation is simpler and faster and involves cutting the sheet of kibbeh into diamonds and then serving. The second method involves rolling the kibbeh into cones and then deep-frying them for additional flavor. This recipe follows the first method.

INGREDIENTS

- 2 cups dried burghul (finely cracked wheat). Yields 4 cups soaked.
- 2 cups ground beef
- 1 cup finely chopped onions
- 2½ teaspoons kibbeh spices
- 2 teaspoons salt

INGREDIENTS FOR YOGURT DIP

- 2 cups yogurt
- 1 cups chopped cucumber
- ½ teaspoon chopped garlic
- 1½ teaspoons salt
- 1 tablespoon dried mint

INGREDIENTS FOR STUFFING

- ¼ cup canola oil
- 4 cups chopped onions
- 2 cups ground meat (lamb or beef)
- 1 teaspoon salt (or ½ tsp if preferred)
- 1½ teaspoons seven-spice blend
- 1 cup pine nuts

PREPARATION

1. Soak the burghul for about 30 minutes in water, then drain it.

2. Place aluminum foil on the bottom of a standard glass baking tray to prevent the meat from sticking to the bottom of the tray. This makes the clean-up process easier.

3. Place the burghul, meat, kibbeh spices, and onions in an electric mixer.

4. Use a flat beater in the electric mixer to smooth the mixture until the ingredients are well incorporated.

5. Split the kibbeh mix in half.

6. Flatten the mix until smooth and add a ¾ inch layer of it to the bottom of the tray.

7. Add the stuffing evenly to form a layer on top of it.

8. Then, grab a handful of the remaining kibbeh mix. Flatten it to the size of your palm.

9. Cover the stuffing in patches, so you have an even, ¾-inch layer on top of the stuffing.

10. When it is all flat, dip your hand in water and smooth the top of the kibbeh.

11. When cutting the kibbeh into the diamond pattern, use a dull knife that has been dipped in water to ensure a smooth cut. This will prevent the kibbeh from crumbling.

12. Place the tray into the oven at 375°F for around 45 minutes to 1 hour.

13. When the recipe is finished, there will likely still be some stuffing left over. This depends on how thick you want the kibbeh stuffing to be and the depth of the tray you have used. The deeper the tray, the more room for stuffing. However, the larger and shallower the tray, the thinner the stuffing will be and the smaller the chance of leftover stuffing. Leftover stuffing can be eaten alone with pita bread or used in omelets.

PREPARATION FOR STUFFING

1. Sautee the chopped onions in a pan until they are golden and translucent.

2. Add the meat and keep turning until the meat is cooked through.

3. Add the pine nuts, the spices and let the mixture cook for a few minutes.

PREPARATION FOR YOGURT

1. Pound or finely chop the garlic in a bowl.

2. Add the salt, cucumbers, and olive oil and mix well.

3. Sprinkle the dried mint on top.

Loubeh Bzeit

4-5 PEOPLE **VEGAN** **45-1hr** **GLUTEN FREE** **LOW FAT**

This dish, along with other recipes in this book, is one of the reasons that the Mediterranean diet is widely regarded as one of the healthiest and most delicious diets in the world. Traditionally, loubeh bzeit is served as a main dish, but it can also be served in smaller portions as a side dish.

INGREDIENTS

- 4 cups chopped green beans (fresh or frozen)
- 2 cups finely chopped onions
- 1 cup coarsely chopped tomatoes
- 5 to 10 whole cloves of fresh garlic
- 2 teaspoons salt
- 2 tablespoons tomato paste
- ½ teaspoon fresh black pepper
- ¼ cup canola oil
- 2 cups water

PREPARATION

1. Start by sautéing the onions in the canola oil. Once they become golden and translucent, add the tomatoes, stir, and then cover.

2. After 5 minutes, add the green beans, stir, and then cover for another 5 to 10 minutes.

3. Uncover and add the garlic cloves, salt, and pepper. Re-cover.

4. In a separate bowl, stir the tomato paste into the water.

5. Once blended, pour over the green beans.

6. Stir the mixture, cover, and bring to a boil for 10 minutes.

7. Uncover, stir, lower the heat, and let simmer. Cook for another 10 minutes. Re-cover.

8. Uncover, stir, turn up the heat to high for 1 minute, and then turn the heat off.

9. Leave the pot on the stove and keep covered for 30 to 45 minutes.

Mussakhan Tortilla Rolls

PREPARATION

1. Sauté the onions in the canola oil until golden, usually for about 5 to 10 minutes.

2. Add the shredded chicken and stir for about 2 to 5 minutes until the mixture is warm/hot to the touch. Feel free to further chop the chicken pieces if you like a finer texture. I usually like to keep them large.

3. Add the sumac, za'atar, pepper, and salt. Stir and allow the mix to cook for 2 minutes.

4. On the side, prepare the tortillas by laying them out on a tray. This makes it easier to scoop the meat and vegetables from the stove onto the open tortillas. If you choose to make larger rolls, you can use larger tortillas and portion larger amounts of mixture into the rolls. Smaller tortillas will make more rolls and work better as a snack.

An easy mom saver that can use prebaked rotisserie chicken that is pulled apart and cooked with onions and sumac. Getting the kids involved with rolling the tortillas is a fun way to get them interested and active in the kitchen and helps bring the family together. This is a wonderful option for a quick lunch or dinner and is a guaranteed favorite of kids of all ages.

 **5-10 PEOPLE**  **45 min - 1 hr**  **LOW FAT**

INGREDIENTS

- 3 cups shredded rotisserie chicken
- 3 cups finely chopped onions
- ½ cup canola oil
- 20 medium-sized flour tortillas
- 2 tablespoons sumac
- ½ tablespoon za'atar
- 1 teaspoon salt
- ¼ teaspoon fresh black pepper (adjust to taste)

5. After 2 minutes, turn off the heat.

6. Place about 2 tablespoons in every tortilla and then roll.

7. Spray the bottom of a glass baking tray with nonstick cooking spray.

8. Place the rolls snugly in the tray.

9. Spray one side of a sheet of aluminum foil with nonstick cooking spray and cover the tray. Make sure the sprayed side is facing down toward the tortillas. This will prevent the rolls from tearing open when you remove the foil.

10. Bake in the oven at 375°F for 15 minutes or until the tops of the tortillas are golden brown.

SIDE DISHES

Unique, colorful companions ▶ ▶ ▶ to every dish.

01. Hummus

An essential part of Lebanese cuisine. Packed with proteins and nutrients, this dish can be paired with almost anything. Talk about healthy meal prep! Hummus can be eaten at breakfast, lunch, or dinner and can be served as a side or snack.

Side Dishes

02. Brussels Sprouts

A side dish that's easy on the eyes and the stomach. This recipe uses three simple ingredients for a bright, new, Mediterranean taste. Low-fat and guilt-free, especially with turkey bacon. This dish reheats very well and is an excellent choice for meal prep.

03. Egg and Sausage Vegetable Salad

A light and refreshing vegetable and protein salad that can be made quickly. Often used as a side for grilled meats in Lebanese culture, this dish is served cold and packed with color and fresh taste.

04. Garlic Mashed Potatoes

An emboldened take on the common American side dish. This recipe is vegan and gluten-free but manages to pack in all the soft, comfy goodness of the original.

05. Mediterranean Orzo Pasta Salad

A flexible and fresh summer dish that can be served as a vegetarian side or paired with a protein as part of the main course. This recipe is served cold, making it the perfect option for meal prep or a quick go-to for lunches and dinners.

06. French Green Bean Salad

This Mediterranean twist on a French classic is not only nutritious but quick to prepare and budget friendly. A perfect side dish for college students or for a mom who's always on the move. Provides health and bushels of vitamins in a delectable, vegan and gluten-free bundle!

Hummus

This highly delicious and adaptable recipe can open a whole new world of meal opportunities. Whether it's used as a vegetable or pita dip or as a side dish for your main course, this is an absolute must-have at a moment's notice.

2-3 PEOPLE

VEGAN

30 min

GLUTEN FREE

LOW FAT

INGREDIENTS

- 1 can (15 ounces) chickpeas or 1½ cups of cooked chickpeas
- ¼ cup lemon juice
- ½ tablespoon chopped garlic
- ½ teaspoon salt
- ½ cup tahini (hulled sesame-seed butter)
- 2 to 4 tablespoons ice water (more as needed)

INGREDIENTS FOR GARNISH

- Fresh parsley leaves
- Mint
- Carrots
- Tomatoes

OR

- Paprika
- A drizzle of olive oil

PREPARATION

1. In a food processor or high-powered blender, combine the lemon juice, tahini, garlic, and salt. Process until the mixture is smooth.

2. Scrape out any tahini stuck to the sides and bottom of the processor if necessary.

3. Add the chickpeas and continue processing.

4. While running the food processor, drizzle in 2 tablespoons of ice water.

5. Scrape out the food processor and blend until the mixture is ultra-smooth, pale, and creamy. If your tahini was extra-thick to begin with, you may need to add 1 or 2 more tablespoons of ice water.

6. Taste and adjust as necessary. I almost always add another ¼ teaspoon salt for more flavor and another tablespoon of lemon juice for extra zing.

7. Scrape the hummus into a serving bowl or platter and use the back of a spoon to create a smooth, swirled pattern on top.

8. Top with garnishes of your choice and serve. If covered, leftover hummus keeps well in the refrigerator for up to 1 week.

Brussels Sprouts

PREPARATION

1. In a pan or a large skillet, add the canola oil.

2. Once the oil is hot, add the brussels sprouts.

3. Cover the pan and let them cook on medium to medium-high heat for a few minutes.

4. Toss the vegetables and taste test until they have a consistency that you like.

5. Once ready, add the finely chopped, cooked turkey bacon. Feel free to replace it with real bacon if desired.

6. Toss for 1 to 2 minutes, then add the roasted pine nuts. Remove from the skillet and place in a bowl.

7. Add the extra-virgin olive oil, balsamic vinegar, salt, and pepper to taste. Mix well and serve immediately.

4-5 PEOPLE

30-45 min

GLUTEN FREE

LOW FAT

Discover a new twist to an old, boring vegetable. This recipe makes brussels sprouts crispy, caramelized, and absolutely addictive. The Lebanese influence in this recipe creates a mouthwatering flavor that will never again leave you dreading brussels sprouts. This dish reheats well without the sprouts becoming chewy or soggy so it is ideal to serve again, if you manage to leave any leftovers.

INGREDIENTS

- 4 cups trimmed and halved brussels sprouts
- 2 tablespoons canola oil
- ½ teaspoon kosher salt (adjust to taste)
- ¼ teaspoon black pepper (adjust to taste)
- 1½ tablespoons balsamic vinegar
- 2 tablespoons extra-virgin olive oil
- ½ cup chopped, cooked turkey bacon
- ¼ cup roasted pine nuts

Egg and Sausage Vegetable Salad

This Mediterranean version of salad russe is a filling and healthy side dish that packs in vibrant flavor and healthy ingredients. This recipe introduces a wide variety of Lebanese-inspired ingredients that can liven up your dinner table with their vivid colors and provide a healthier, more flavorful alternative to your usual salad mix.

INGREDIENTS

- 1 can (15¼ ounces) sweet corn
- 1 can (15¼ ounces) julienned beets
- 1 can (15¼ ounces) sweet peas
- 2 cups chopped turkey hotdogs
- ¼ cup finely chopped pickles (Armenian cucumber pickles recommended)
- ¼ teaspoon onion powder
- ¼ teaspoon garlic powder
- ¼ teaspoon salt
- ¼ teaspoon pepper
- 3 tablespoons mayonnaise
- 2 hard-boiled eggs

4-5 PEOPLE

1 hr

GLUTEN FREE

PREPARATION

1. Ingredients should be prepared in advance, especially the hotdogs, which should be cooked in whatever manner you prefer.

2. Slice the hard-boiled eggs into wedges and set aside.

3. Drain the canned vegetables and mix into a bowl.

4. Incorporate the remaining ingredients into one dish and place the hard-boiled eggs around or over the plate or bowl. Voilà! You are done!

Garlic Mashed Potatoes

This recipe introduces additional flavor to the traditional dish. The incorporation of extra-virgin olive oil gives the potatoes a richer flavor and texture. This small twist allows you to liven up the simple side without sacrificing any of its warmth or comfort. It is ideal for any gathering or family dinner.

INGREDIENTS

- 4 cups of chopped russet potatoes pieces
- 1 tablespoon pressed garlic
- ⅔ cup extra-virgin olive oil
- 1 teaspoon salt

INGREDIENTS FOR GARNISH

- 1 teaspoon dried mint

2-3 PEOPLE

VEGAN

30 min

GLUTEN FREE

LOW FAT

PREPARATION

1. Peel the potatoes and cut into large pieces.

2. Place in a pot and add water. The water should be about an inch over the potatoes.

3. Sprinkle a little salt into the water and cover the pot.

4. Bring to a boil.

5. Cook for about 10 minutes or until the potatoes are tender. At this point, they should slide off of a fork.

6. While the potatoes are cooking, use a mortar and pestle to press the garlic.

7. Once the potatoes are cooked, drain the potatoes and let them rest in a strainer for another 10 minutes.

8. Once they are sufficiently drained and cool to the touch, move the potatoes into an appropriately sized bowl.

9. Add the garlic and the olive oil and smash with a potato ricer or a large fork. Make sure to hand mix these ingredients and refrain from using any electric mixers as they will make the potatoes gummy. This is because the blades in an electric mixer separate and tear the starch molecules.

10. Serve immediately or pack for meal prep.

Mediterranean Orzo Pasta Salad

This recipe is vibrant, zesty, fresh, and satisfying. This dish is perfect for a summer or spring luncheon and can serve as an alternative to the simpler, more uniform pasta salads that people expect. Be careful, though, as bringing this to a get-together could have guests or friends begging you to make it for them again.

INGREDIENTS

- 1 cup orzo (yields 3 cups cooked)
- 2 tablespoons extra-virgin olive oil
- 1 tablespoon balsamic vinaigrette
- 3 teaspoons fresh basil or basil flakes
- 1 teaspoon salt
- ¼ teaspoon black pepper
- 1 tablespoon lemon juice
- 1 cup chopped tomatoes
- ¼ cup finely chopped onions (try red onions for a burst of color)
- 1 can (15¼ ounces) cut whole-kernel corn

OPTIONAL INGREDIENTS

- 1 pouch (6.4 ounces) tuna
- 1 cup freshly cooked tilapia, shredded

4-5 PEOPLE

30 - 45 min

LOW FAT

VEGAN

PREPARATION

1. Prepare the orzo according to the directions on the box.

2. Add a little salt and a drizzle of extra-virgin olive oil to the boiling water.

3. Once cooked, drain the orzo in a strainer and pour into a bowl.

4. In a separate container, prepare the dressing by mixing the olive oil, balsamic vinegar, lemon juice, salt, and pepper.

5. Add the tomatoes, onions, and corn to the orzo.

6. Pour the dressing over the vegetables and mix.

7. Add the fresh basil or basil flakes if fresh basil is not available.

8. For a nonvegan or nonvegetarian option, feel free to add tuna or freshly cooked tilapia.

9. Break apart into small pieces before adding to the salad.

French Green Bean Salad

4-5 PEOPLE

GLUTEN FREE

30 min

LOW FAT

VEGAN

This delicious side dish will make you wish it was the main course. Although simple, this recipe serves as a reminder that not all great dishes come in complicated packages. It is served cold and elevates the typically dull flavor of green beans with a variety of ingredients inspired by Mediterranean cuisine.

INGREDIENTS

- 4 cans (58 ounces) French-cut green beans
- 1 tablespoon crushed garlic
- 1 teaspoon salt
- ⅓ cup lemon juice
- ¼ cup tahini (hulled sesame-seed butter)
- ⅓ cup olive oil
- 1 cup walnuts (whole or crushed)

PREPARATION

1. Drain the cans of green beans and place the green beans into a bowl.

2. Mix in the lemon juice and olive oil.

3. Incorporate the garlic, salt, and tahini (or substitute) into the bowl.

4. If the walnuts are crushed, stir a portion of them into the mixture.

5. Top with the walnuts or mix them in.

6. Place the mixture into a serving dish.

SWEETS

An exotic collection to satisfy
▶ ▶ ▶ anyone's sweet tooth.

01. Strawberry Muffins

These provide a delicious twist on common blueberry muffins with an intense flavor that can go from sweet to sour in a bite. The sugar on the top gives the muffins a golden hue that breaks open into a bright red berry flavor. Perfect for meal prep, lunch boxes, and a late morning on the go!

Sweets

02. Baklawa

This dish is a nut-filled pastry topped with orange-blossom syrup. The recipe uses Lebanese staples to create a sweet and satisfying treat. A bit of protein from the mix of nuts and a bit of sweetness from the orange-blossom syrup blend together to create a melt-in-your-mouth taste without the guilt.

03. Namoura Mini Cakes

This revitalized recipe uses a healthier set of ingredients than the traditional one. It is made using semolina flour and far less sugar and butter than in other variations. This vegetarian dish derives most of its rich flavor and texture from aerated yogurt. Sweet, healthy, and delicious to enjoy on the go. No plates needed.

04. Sfouf

This simple recipe is easy to prepare and can be eaten in a variety of ways. It is not as sweet as other dishes, but it is healthy and pairs excellently with a variety of teas and coffees.

05. Tres Leches Cake

This recipe, like the Chicken Taco Soup, comes from Mexico. After experimenting with a variety of versions for years, I have found that this method of preparation is the most reliable. It is simple yet rich in flavor. This recipe highlights the creamy, cool taste of tres leches and makes it easy to prepare.

06. Ghraybeh Cookies

These light, soft cookies can be prepared in a wide variety of shapes. They are reminiscent of shortbread but provide a more distinctly Lebanese flavor with the use of nuts and ghee, a form of clarified butter that is used in many Mediterranean recipes.

Strawberry Muffins

PREPARATION

1. Preheat the oven to 350°F.

2. Line a 12-cup muffin tin with paper liners.

3. In a medium-sized bowl, sift together the flour, baking powder, and salt.

4. In the bowl of an electric mixer, beat the butter and granulated sugar for about 2 minutes. Add the eggs one at a time, scraping the sides of the bowl and beating well after each addition.

5. Mix in the vanilla extract and almond extract. The batter may look grainy, but that is okay.

6. With the mixer on low, add the flour mixture in 3 separate pours, alternating with the milk.

7. Set aside ½ cup of strawberries before gradually incorporating the berries into the batter using 2 teaspoons of flour. The flour will prevent them from sinking to the bottom of the mixture.

8. Finish adding the strawberries to the batter and fold with a spatula until evenly distributed. Do not overmix!

9. Scoop the batter into the prepared muffin tin (an ice-cream scoop with a wire scraper works well here). They will be very full.

These muffins are a terrific way to utilize those uneaten strawberries that are sitting in the fridge. They also provide a new inspiration to take some friends or family strawberry picking! Gather together to bake and prepare the strawberries you picked yourself and then enjoy this wonderful treat. They are easily frozen and can be stored for up to 3 months.

INGREDIENTS

- 2 cups all-purpose flour
- ½ teaspoon all-purpose flour for tossing with strawberries
- 2 teaspoons baking powder
- ¾ teaspoon salt
- 1 stick (½ cup) unsalted, softened butter
- 1 cup granulated sugar
- 2 large eggs
- 1½ teaspoons vanilla extract
- ½ cup milk
- 2¼ cups diced strawberries
- 2 tablespoons brown sugar

12-14 CUPCAKES

30 min - 1 hr

10. Scatter the remaining berries evenly over the muffins, then sprinkle the brown sugar evenly on top of each muffin.

11. Bake for about 30 minutes.

12. If you want to give the muffins an extra-golden hue, turn off the oven after they are baked and let them rest for 15 to 20 minutes.

13. Take out and cool in the pan for about 25 minutes.

14. Transfer the muffins to a rack to cool completely.

15. After they are completely cooled, serve or store.

16. If you freeze the muffins, double wrap them securely with aluminum foil or plastic freezer wrap or place in a heavy-duty freezer bag.

17. Thaw overnight on the countertop before eating.

Baklawa

10-20 PIECES

30 min - 1 hr

This traditional Lebanese dessert is revitalized with this recipe. All the crispy, crunchy, golden goodness of the filo-pastry layers deliciously sandwich in the walnuts, pistachios, or cashews. If stored after baking, double wrap the baklawa in plastic wrap before freezing and allow it to thaw overnight on the countertop before serving.

INGREDIENTS

- 1 roll filo dough
- 2 cups finely crushed walnuts (substitute with unsalted pistachios or cashews)
- ½ cup sugar
- ½ teaspoon cinnamon
- ½ cup (1 stick) unsalted butter
- ½ cup canola oil
- ¼ cup finely crushed pistachios
- 1 cup orange-blossom syrup (see recipe on page 65)

PREPARATION

1. Remove the filo roll from the freezer and leave it on the countertop for about 3 to 4 hours.

2. After that time has passed, unroll and split in half.

3. Spray the bottom of a flat tray with a nonstick cooking spray and take the top half of the filo-dough layer and lay it down.

4. In a mortar or a food processor, mix the walnuts with the sugar and cinnamon and, when fully blended, lay the mixture on top of the filo dough in an even layer. The size and thickness of the crushed walnuts can be adjusted to your preference.

5. Then lay the other half of the filo sheets on top of the nuts.

6. With a serrated knife, slowly cut the dough into the desired shapes. Typically, it is cut into diamonds or squares. You might have to gently hold onto the top filo layer to keep it from drifting.

7. In another bowl, melt the butter in the microwave for about 30 seconds. Stir until there are no solid pieces.

8. Add the canola oil to the butter and blend thoroughly.

9. When ready, spoon the canola and butter mixture on top of the baklawa, making sure it soaks through evenly. Again, this is where you can use as much or as little as you want.

10. Bake at 350°F for 20 to 25 minutes. When the baklawa is golden, remove it from the oven and immediately drizzle the orange blossom syrup on top as evenly as you can. Add as much as you feel is needed.

11. Make sure to let it cool for at least 3 hours. Then decorate with the finely crushed pistachios.

Namoura Mini Cakes

PREPARATION FOR CAKES

1. Melt the butter in the microwave in 30-second increments. Make sure to stir in between and be mindful that the butter doesn't get too hot and doesn't bubble.

2. Place the semolina, melted butter, sugar, milk, and baking powder in a large bowl and stir until well combined. Set aside for 1 hour.

3. After 45 minutes have passed, in another bowl, mix the yogurt with the baking soda, and let it sit for 15 minutes or until it doubles in size.

4. Pour the yogurt mixture over the semolina mixture and mix well to combine.

5. Then, using an ice cream scooper, place the mixture into lined cupcake trays.

6. Decorate with almond slivers or with coconut flakes.

7. Let the mixture rest in the cupcake trays for 30 minutes, then bake for 15 minutes at 350°F.

8. After turning the oven off, leave the mini cakes in the oven untouched for 5minutes to let their tops develop a golden hue.

9. Remove from the oven and immediately drizzle one tablespoon of syrup on top of every mini cake.

10. Let them cool completely before removing them from the tray.

Indulge your taste buds in these mini cakes soaked in orange-blossom sugar syrup. So delicious you'll find it easy to clean your plate without even noticing. A great dish to pair with tea or to offer to guests and friends!

INGREDIENTS

- 1½ sticks (¾ cup) of unsalted butter
- 3 cups semolina flour
- ¾ cup granulated sugar
- 1 cup plain whole-milk yogurt
- 2 teaspoons baking soda
- ¼ cup slivered almonds (substitute with coconut flakes if desired)
- ½ cup milk
- 1 teaspoon baking powder

INGREDIENTS FOR SYRUP

- 2 cups granulated sugar
- 1 cup water
- 1 tablespoon freshly squeezed lemon juice
- 1½ teaspoons orange-blossom water (substitute with rose water if unavailable)

12-14 MINICAKES

1-2 hrs

PREPARATION FOR SYRUP

1. In a small saucepan over high heat, boil sugar and orange-blossom water (or substitute), stirring for about 2 minutes or until the sugar is dissolved.

2. Reduce the heat to a simmer, add lemon juice, and stir for another 2 minutes to combine.

3. Remove from the heat and set aside to cool.

4. As the liquid cools, it will thicken to syrup consistency. You can prepare this the day before or ahead of time as it keeps well in the refrigerator and will not harden if covered.

Sfouf

18-20 PEOPLE	45 min	VEGAN

Before the rest of the world knew the full benefits of turmeric, the Lebanese had this turmeric cake called sfouf. The word sfouf means "lines" and refers to the way bakeries stack these not-so-sweet cakes. This dessert can be enjoyed much like a scone, with coffee and tea, or can be eaten alone. This recipe makes 1 medium cake and 12 cupcakes.

INGREDIENTS

- 2 cups all-purpose flour
- 2 cups fine semolina flour
- 3 cups organic, fine sugar (2½ cups if you prefer it to be less sweet)
- 2 cups milk or 2 cups almond milk for a vegan version
- 2 teaspoons baking powder
- 3 teaspoons turmeric powder
- A few raw almonds
- A sprinkle of sesame seeds

PREPARATION

1. Preheat the oven to 350°F.

2. Sift all the dry ingredients and then mix together in a bowl.

3. Mix the wet ingredients in a separate bowl.

4. Combine the wet and dry ingredients for 5 minutes or until they are well incorporated.

5. Pour mixture into a cupcake tray until full, then fill a small cake tray with the remaining ingredients if desired.

6. Bake for 25 to 35 minutes or until a wooden toothpick inserted in the center comes out dry.

7. Gently press almonds into the top of the cupcakes, using as many or as few as desired. Sprinkle sesame seeds on top of the larger cake.

8. Let the cakes rest and fully cool before cutting.

Tres Leches Cake

This traditional Mexican dish has been reinvented often, but I have found that some of the most basic variations are the most reliable. This recipe preserves the simple yet delectable taste of the three-milk cake. The glorious goodness of the soaked cake combined with the cool, refreshing whipped-cream topping makes it an ideal sweet for those long, hot summer days.

INGREDIENTS FOR CAKE

- 1 cup all-purpose flour
- 1½ teaspoons baking powder
- ¼ teaspoon salt
- 5 eggs
- 1 cup sugar
- 1 teaspoon vanilla extract
- ¾ cup unsalted butter
- ⅓ cup whole milk
- ⅓ cup canola oil

INGREDIENTS FOR CAKE TOPPING

- Whipped cream
- Sprinkles of any variety (chocolate sprinkles are recommended)

INGREDIENTS FOR THE 3 MILK SOAK

- 1¼ cups evaporated milk
- ¾ cup sweetened condensed milk
- ⅓ cup heavy whipping cream

 4-5 PEOPLE  1-2 Hrs

PREPARATION

1. Sift the flour and baking powder together and set aside.

2. Cream the butter, sugar, and vanilla together for about 5 to 8 minutes, until fluffy. How long this takes will depend on how soft the butter is. Ideally, it will be room temperature before you use it.

3. Crack the eggs into a separate bowl to keep shell fragments out of the batter . Add a sprinkle of salt and beat with a whisk for a few minutes.

4. Mix the milk and oil together and set aside.

5. Add the flour mixture to the butter mixture 2 tablespoons at a time, alternating between the milk and canola-oil mix until well blended.

6. Pour into the prepared tray and bake at 350°F for 30 minutes.

7. Cover or store in a container overnight and make sure to refrigerate it.

8. The next day, mix the three kinds of milk together, pour over the cake, and let it soak. Let the cake rest in the fridge in a covered tray for 1 hour before serving.

9. Before serving, top with whipped cream and sprinkles.

Greibeh Cookies

I swear that these melt-in-your-mouth cookies have the ability to transport me back to Lebanon. As one of my mother's favorite recipes, it has accompanied me throughout my life. These cookies are made from simple ingredients blended together to create a powerful taste. They are perfect to keep for weeks on end and are enjoyed by young and old alike.

INGREDIENTS

- 5 cups sifted all-purpose flour
- 2 cups sifted confectioners' sugar
- 2 cups ghee at room temperature, not melted or any butter flavor All vegetable shortening
- 28 whole unshelled pistachios

PREPARATION

1. In an electric mixer on low speed, use a flat beater to mix the ghee or ghee substitute with the powdered sugar for 5 minutes.

2. Switch the stand-mixer attachment to a dough hook and start to slowly add the sifted flour. Mix on low to medium speed for about 10 to 20 minutes until it is well incorporated. At first it will look dry, but as it mixes it will start to combine, thicken, and pull away from the sides of the bowl.

3. Scrape the sides every few minutes to ensure the ingredients are mixing evenly. You will know the dough is done when it has the appearance and consistency of playdough.

4. If the temperature in your kitchen is too high, transfer the dough to a sealable plastic bag or wrap with plastic wrap and refrigerate for 20 minutes to allow it to cool.

5. Once you have made the dough and it is cooled, form the dough into balls. Use a small cookie scoop to portion the cookies into 1- to 1½-inch balls.

6. Then, roll the dough in between the palms of your hands to make a small, snakelike shape that is as tall as the width of your hand.

7. Connect the two ends of the dough to form a circle. Or make into plain round shapes.

8. Place a pistachio at the point where the dough connects or in the center of the round shapes.

9. Bake. These cookies bake at a low-temperature heat of 325°F for 15 minutes.

10. Remove from the oven and serve.

Meet the Author

Nassab Ahmadie lives in Evans, Georgia with her husband, three kids, and two cats. When she isn't cooking and baking in her kitchen, she is teaching group fitness and working as a personal trainer. She also does freelance work as a graphic designer and photographer. Throughout the past fifteen years, she has been actively involved in a variety of charities. She also loves diamond art, travel, running, and hiking.

To learn more, visit the following:
Her online portfolio: **NassabAhmadie.com**
Her photography website: **Magnificent3Photography.com**
Her latest charitable venture: **Beytna.Foundation**

Notes

Notes

Notes

CPSIA information can be obtained
at www.ICGtesting.com
Printed in the USA
BVHW062302211022
650029BV00002B/33

* 9 7 9 8 8 8 5 9 0 9 9 8 3 *